W9-BUA-141

Weirder and CUTER

Luna Moth

by E. Merwin

Consultant: Darin Collins, DVM
Director, Animal Health Programs
Woodland Park Zoo
Seattle, Washington

BEARPORT PUBLISHING

New York, New York

Credits

Cover, © StevenRussellSmithPhotos/Shutterstock; TOC, © StevenRussellSmithPhotos/Shutterstock; 4–5, © Rolf Nussbaumer/Minden; 6L, © happymay/Shutterstock; 6–7, © Cathy Keifer/Dreamstime; 8–9, © Grant Heilman Photography/Alamy Stock Photo; 10T, © Jeff Lepore/Science Source; 10B, © Danita Delimont/Alamy Stock Photo; 11, © Dwight Kuhn; 12, © Dwight Kuhn; 13, © Dwight Kuhn; 14, © Dwight Kuhn; 15, © Papilio/Alamy Stock Photo; 16, © James Laurie/Shutterstock; 17T, © Kirsanov Valeriy Vladimirovich/Shutterstock; 17B, © Gary Corbett/age fotostock/Alamy Stock Photo; 18–19, © StevenRussellSmithPhotos/Shutterstock; 19R, © IrinaK/Shutterstock; 20–21, © Gianpiero Ferrari/Minden; 22 (T to B), © Serguei Koultchitskii/Shutterstock, © Jiri Hodecek/Shutterstock, and © Dr. Arthur Anker; 23TL, © Brenda McGee-Paap/Shutterstock; 23TR, © Geoffrey Kuchera/Shutterstock; 23BL, © wagtail/Shutterstock; 23BR, © StevenRussellSmithPhotos/Shutterstock; Back Cover, © StudioOneNine/Shutterstock.

Publisher: Kenn Goin
Senior Editor: Joyce Tavolacci
Creative Director: Spencer Brinker
Design: Debrah Kaiser
Photo Researcher: Thomas Persano

Library of Congress Cataloging-in-Publication Data

Names: Merwin, E., author.
Title: Luna moth / by E. Merwin.
Description: New York, New York : Bearport Publishing, [2018] | Series:
   Weirder and cuter | Includes bibliographical references and index. |
   Audience: Ages 5–8.
Identifiers: LCCN 2017005089 (print) | LCCN 2017016278 (ebook) |
ISBN 9781684023134 (ebook) | ISBN 9781684022595 (library)
Subjects: LCSH: Luna moth—Juvenile literature. | Luna moth—Life
   cycles—Juvenile literature. | Moths—Juvenile literature.
Classification: LCC QL561.S2 (ebook) | LCC QL561.S2 M47 2018 (print) | DDC
   595.78—dc23
LC record available at https://lccn.loc.gov/2017005089

For more information, write to Bearport Publishing Company, Inc., 45 West 21st Street, Suite 3B, New York, New York 10010. Printed in the United States of America.

10 9 8 7 6 5 4 3 2 1

Contents

Luna Moth.................4

More Weird Moths.................22

Glossary.........................23

Index 24

Read More 24

Learn More Online 24

About the Author 24

What's this weird
but cute animal?

It's a
luna moth.

White **fuzzy** body!

Fluttering **lime-green** wings!

5

A luna moth is an **insect** with huge wings.

Its wingspan is 4 to 5 inches (10 to 13 cm).

That's about the width of a grown-up's hand!

frilly tail

Each of the luna moth's wings has a long, frilly tail.

Poking out of the moth's head are two yellow **antennae**.

They look like feathery combs.

Moths use their antennae to feel and to smell.

male luna moth

A male luna moth can sniff out a female from 7 miles (11 km) away!

A moth's life begins as an egg.

After the egg hatches, a hungry caterpillar crawls out.

egg

caterpillar

Munch, munch, munch.

It gobbles up lots of leaves!

caterpillar

Luna moths live in forests in North America.

After a month, the chubby caterpillar spins a **cocoon**.

It wraps itself up in silk and leaves.

cocoon

About three weeks later, an adult moth wiggles out!

moth

cocoon

Before a moth hatches from its cocoon, it's called a pupa.

At first, the luna moth's wings are damp and crumpled.

Soon, they dry and unfold.

Now, the moth is ready to flutter through the forest.

Luna moths, like most moths, fly only at night.

Watch out! Bats love to eat luna moths.

The insects have a way to esape, though.

They spin their long tail **tendrils**.

This motion confuses the bats.

bat

Then the moths can fly away!

A luna moth can still fly even if its tendrils are damaged.

Luna moths have
four dark spots
on their wings.

These spots
look like big eyes.

Boo! They scare away other enemies, such as birds.

The color of a luna moth's wings also keep it safe. Its green wings blend in with leaves. This helps the insect hide.

An adult luna moth never takes a bite of food.

Why?

This insect has no mouth or stomach!

An adult luna moth lives for only one week.

21

More Weird Moths

Comet Moth
With 10-inch (25 cm) wings, it's one of the world's largest moths. Like the luna moth, its adult life is short—less than one week!

Death's Head Hawkmoth
This moth is named for the spot on its back that looks like a skull. If you poke a death's head hawkmoth, it will squeak!

Venezuelan Poodle Moth
This fuzzy moth is small enough to sit on the tip of your finger! Its body is covered with thick, white hair. Its hair is so thick that it's hard for enemies to swallow it.

Glossary

antennae (an-TEN-ee) the two body parts on an insect's head used for feeling and smelling

cocoon (kuh-KOON) a silky covering that some insects make to protect their bodies while they grow

insect (IN-sekt) a small animal that has six legs, three main body parts, two antennae, and a hard covering

tendrils (TEN-drilz) long, thin stem-like body parts

Index

antennae 8–9

caterpillar 10–11, 12

cocoon 12–13

eye spots 18–19

food 10–11, 20

pupa 13

size 6, 22

wings 4–5, 6–7, 14, 18–19, 22

Read More

Himmelman, John. *A Luna Moth's Life.* New York: Children's Press (1998).

Markle, Sandra. *Luna Moths: Masters of Change.* Minneapolis, MN: Lerner (2008).

Learn More Online

To learn more about luna moths, visit **www.bearportpublishing.com/WeirderAndCuter**

About the Author

E. Merwin enjoys the wonders of nature. Having spent many summer nights capturing (and letting go of) fireflies, she has a great admiration for winged insects.